FABULOUS ANIMALS

The Story of the Platypus

Anita Ganeri

capstone

Edited by Linda Staniford
Designed by Philippa Jenkins
Original illustrations © Capstone Global Library Limited 2016
Picture research by Morgan Walters
Production by Victoria Fitzgerald
Originated by Capstone Global Library Ltd
Printed and bound in China

19 18 17 16 15
10 9 8 7 6 5 4 3 2 1

Library of Congress Cataloging-in-Publication Data
Cataloging-in-publication information is on file with the Library of Congress.
Written by Anita Ganeri
ISBN 978-1-4846-2710-5 (hardcover)
ISBN 978-1-4846-2714-3 (paperback)
ISBN 978-1-4846-2718-1 (eBook PDF)

Acknowledgments
The author and publisher are grateful to the following for permission to reproduce copyright material: Alamy: INTERFOTO, 20, jackie ellis, 26, Kevin Wells, 12; Bridgeman Images: Nockels, David (20th century)/Private Collection /Look and Learn, 18; Getty Images: De Agostini Picture Library, 8; National Geographic Creative: JASON EDWARDS, 23; Newscom: D. Parer & E. Parer-Cook, 17, MICK TSIKAS/REUTERS, 15, Roland Seitre/Minden Pictures, 6, Roland Seitre/D. Parer & E. Parer-Cook/Minden Pictures, 16; Rebecca Pian, 27; Science Source: Jean-Philippe Varin, 19; Shutterstock: Aksenova Natalya, (duck head) 5, Curioso, (otter body) 5, Eric Isselee, (snake) bottom 7, Jagodka, (ferret) top 7, John Carnemolla, 9, Kletr, 25, kwest, 24, panbazil, (duck) middle 7; SuperStock: Minden Pictures, 13, NHPA, Cover, 10, 14, Universal Images Group, 11; Wikimedia: Freeman.pdf, 21, Wellcome Images, 4.

We would like to thank Michael Bright for his invaluable help in the preparation of this book.

Every effort has been made to contact copyright holders of any material reproduced in this book. Any omissions will be rectified in subsequent printings if notice is given to the publisher.

All the Internet addresses (URLs) given in this book were valid at the time of going to press. However, due to the dynamic nature of the Internet, some addresses may have changed, or sites may have changed or ceased to exist since publication. While the author and publisher regret any inconvenience this may cause readers, no responsibility for any such changes can be accepted by either the author or the publisher.

Contents

Mystery Animal.................................4

A New Animal?.............................8

Local Knowledge.......................10

Meet the Platypus...................12

Platypus Lifestyle....................14

In Captivity...............................20

Platypuses Today....................24

Platypus Timeline..................28

Glossary................................30

Find Out More.......................31

Index....................................32

Some words are shown in bold, like this. You can find out what they mean by looking in the glossary.

Mystery Animal

In the 1700s, people from Great Britain began to settle in Australia. They saw many strange animals. Captain John Hunter was **governor** of New South Wales. In 1798, he sent the skin of an extraordinary animal back to England.

Pub.d by FF Nodder June 1799.

This is an early drawing of a platypus.

What sort of
animal was this?

Scientists were puzzled. They thought that the
animal must be a fake. It looked as if someone
had sewn a duck's bill onto a **miniature**
otter's body, with fur from a beaver.

More skins and skulls arrived from Australia. Scientists studied them carefully. They soon saw that this was a real animal after all. They called it the "platypus," which means "flat-footed," after its webbed feet.

A platypus has webbed feet for swimming.

For years, scientists tried to figure out what kind of animal it was.
It had fur like a **mammal**.

It had a bill like a bird.

It laid eggs like a bird or a **reptile**.

The scientists could not agree which group it fit into.

A New Animal?

In 1883, a Scottish scientist, William Caldwell, arrived in Australia. He searched for platypus eggs and nests. He also caught a female that made milk for her babies. This proved that the platypus was a **monotreme**-a **mammal** that laid eggs.

This female platypus is in her nest with her eggs.

Like platypuses, echidnas are mammals that lay eggs.

Mammals are animals with fur or hair. They feed their babies on milk. Most mammals give birth to live babies, but platypus babies hatch from eggs. The only other kind of monotremes are echidnas (spiny anteaters).

Local Knowledge

Long before the Europeans came, the **indigenous** Australians hunted platypuses for their meat. They caught them in the water, using spears. Later, they helped scientists to look for platypuses.

A platypus comes out of its burrow.

This is an indigenous Australian painting of a platypus.

The indigenous Australians also told stories about the platypus. One story tells how the mother of the first platypus was a duck. Its father was a water-rat. So, the platypus got its mother's bill and webbed feet, and its father's soft brown fur.

Meet the Platypus

The platypus lives in rivers and streams in eastern Australia. It spends a lot of time in the water, looking for food. It digs burrows in the riverbank, where it rests and makes its nest.

A platypus looks for food in the river.

Male platypuses have spurs on their back legs.

A platypus is about the size of a cat. Males are bigger than females. Males have little pointed **spurs** on their back legs. They use these to jab **venom** into **predators**, such as snakes, rats, and **goannas**.

Platypus Lifestyle

Platypuses are excellent swimmers. They use their webbed feet like paddles. They use their flat tails for steering. They close their eyes and ears underwater. But they have to come to the surface to breathe.

A platypus paddles with its webbed feet.

A platypus's special fur keeps it dry in the water.

A platypus has thick, brown fur on its body. The fur traps air next to its skin. This helps to keep the platypus warm in the water. Its fur is also waterproof.

A platypus eats worms, shrimps, and insect grubs. It uses its bill to dig them up from the muddy riverbed. The platypus stores the food in pouches in its cheeks until it reaches the surface.

A platypus hunts for food on the riverbed.

The platypus's bill
is flat and smooth.

The platypus has special **sensors** in its
bill. It uses the sensors to find its food. Its
prey gives out tiny electrical signals. The
platypus's bill picks these signals up.

In October, the female platypus digs a special burrow in the riverbank. Inside, she builds a nest from grass and leaves. She lays two to three small, soft eggs in the nest. Then she curls around them to keep them warm.

A female platypus lays her eggs in her nest.

A mother platypus cares for her newly hatched babies.

The babies hatch about 10 days later. They have no hair and cannot see. Their mother feeds them on milk. The babies stay in the burrow until they are about four months old.

In Captivity

Scientists caught thousands of platypuses. But it was difficult to keep them alive for long. Then an Australian scientist named Henry Burrell had a brilliant idea.

Scientists explored Australia in the 1800s.

Burrell called
his tank a
"**platypusary.**"

In 1910, Burrell invented a special tank
for keeping platypuses. It had water and a
burrow inside to make the platypuses feel at
home. For the first time, Burrell caught some
platypuses and managed to keep them alive.

Some of the platypuses Henry Burrell caught were put on display at a zoo in Sydney, Australia. Then, in 1922, he helped to send a platypus to the Bronx Zoo in New York. It was the first time a live platypus had been seen outside Australia.

Tickets like this were issued to see the platypuses in New York.

THIS TICKET
ADMITS TWO

00183

Come and see the Duck-billed Platypus!

Members and friends of the New York Zoological Society are invited to attend this exclusive viewing of a Duck-Billed Platypus, in the Platypusary, south of the Elephant House.

Date: Friday, May 19
Time: 2.00pm

The Platypus is the most amazing of all living mammals. It has never before been exhibited alive outside its native Australia.

Early booking is recommended.

These platypus twins were born in captivity.

Today, the only **captive** platypuses live in zoos in Australia. In 1998, a platypus at Healesville Sanctuary in Victoria, Australia, gave birth to twins. They were named Barak and Yarra. These were the first platypus twins to be born in captivity.

Platypuses Today

Today, platypuses still live in eastern Australia. A small group of platypuses also lives on Kangaroo Island in South Australia. It is against the law to catch or trap a platypus.

Platypuses live on Kangaroo Island in Australia.

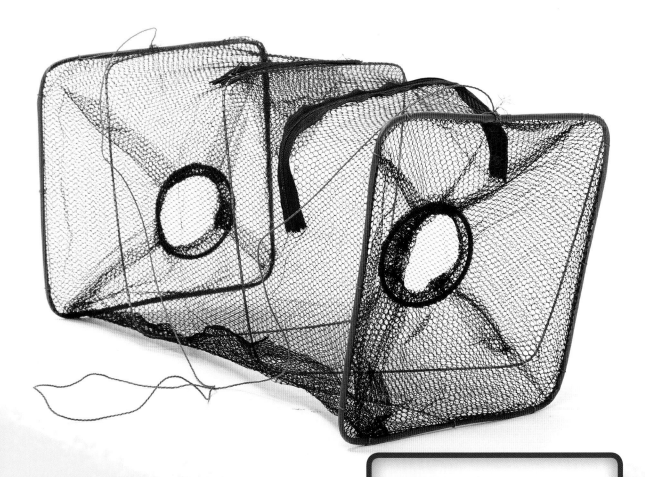

Traps like this are used
for catching yabbies.

Groups such as the Australian Platypus
Conservancy work hard to protect these
amazing animals. One of their projects is
to stop so many platypuses from being
accidentally caught and killed in **yabby** traps.

Scientists are still learning more about the platypus. In the 1980s and 1990s, scientists in Australia figured out how platypuses use the electrical **sensors** in their bills to search for food.

This scientist is on the lookout for platypuses.

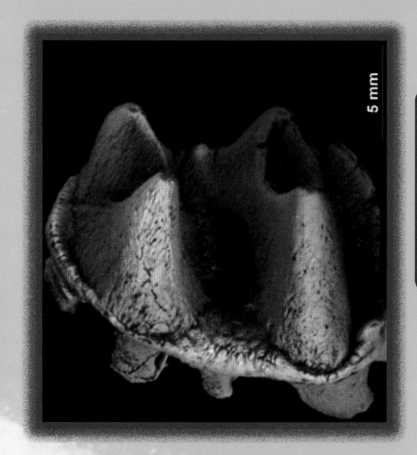

5 mm

This fossil tooth may come from the ancestor of the modern platypus.

In 2012, scientists in Australia found a fossil of a huge platypus tooth. They think that it comes from a giant platypus that lived around 5 to 15 million years ago. It looked similar to a modern platypus, but it was at least twice as big.

Platypus Timeline

1798

John Hunter sends the first platypus skin to England.

1799

George Shaw writes the first scientific description of the platypus.

1803

Étienne Geoffroy St.-Hilaire puts the platypus and echidna into the new animal group of monotremes.

1883/4

William Caldwell finds some platypus eggs, proving that this is an egg-laying mammal.

1910

Henry Burrell invents and builds his "platypusary."

1922

The first platypuses outside Australia arrive at the Bronx Zoo, in New York.

1943

David Fleay breeds "Corrie," the first platypus born in captivity at Healesville Sanctuary, Victoria, Australia.

1986

Scientists discover how the platypus uses its "electrical sense."

1998

The first platypus twins in captivity are born at Healesville Sanctuary.

2012

Scientists find a fossil of a tooth that belonged to a giant ancient platypus.

Glossary

ancestor family member who lived a very long time ago

captive animal that lives in a zoo or wildlife park

goanna type of lizard that lives in Australia

governor official who ran parts of Australia on behalf of the British government

indigenous native to a place

mammal warm-blooded animal that breathes air; mammals have hair or fur; female mammals feed milk to their young

miniature much smaller than usual size

monotreme mammal that lays eggs

platypusary special tank for keeping platypuses

predator animal that hunts other animals for food

prey animal that is hunted by another animal for food

reptile cold-blooded animal that breathes air and has a backbone; most reptiles lay eggs and have scaly skin

sensor part of an animal's body that detects changes in the world around it

spur spine-like bump on a platypus's leg

venom poison injected through an animal's bite or sting

yabby animal like a crayfish that lives in rivers and streams in Australia

Find Out More

Books

Antill, Sara. *Platypus* (Unusual Animals). New York: Windmill Books, 2011.

Leaf, Christina. *Platypus* (Extremely Weird Animals). Minneapolis: Bellwether Media, 2014.

Spilsbury, Richard, and Louise Spilsbury. *Animals in Danger in Australia* (Animals in Danger). Chicago: Heinemann Library, 2013.

Websites

FactHound offers a safe, fun way to find Internet sites related to this book. All of the sites on FactHound have been researched by our staff.

Here's all you do:

Visit www.facthound.com
Type in this code: 9781484627105

Index

Australia 4, 6, 8, 12, 20, 23, 24, 26, 27
Australian Platypus Conservancy 25

babies 8, 9, 19
bill 7, 11, 16, 17, 26
Bronx Zoo, New York 22
Burrell, Henry 20, 21, 22

Caldwell, William 8

echidna 9
eggs 7, 8, 9, 18

fake 5
food 12, 16, 17, 26
fossil platypus 27
fur 5, 7, 11, 15

Healesville Sanctuary, Victoria, Australia 23
Hunter, Captain John 4

indigenous Australians 10, 11

keeping platypuses in zoos 20, 21, 22, 23

mammals 7, 8, 9
monotremes 8, 9

nest 12, 18

platypusary 21, 22
predators 13

size 13
spiny anteater 9
spurs 13
swimming 14

venom 13

webbed feet 6, 11, 14
wild platypuses 24

yabby traps 25